The Happiness Book For Little Christians

A Biblical Guide To Happiness!

By Mike Duffy
and Kendall Duffy

Scripture quotations taken from the New American Standard Bible®,
Copyright © 1960, 1962, 1963, 1968, 1971, 1972, 1973,
1975, 1977, 1995 by The Lockman Foundation
Used by permission." (www.Lockman.org)

THE HOLY BIBLE, NEW INTERNATIONAL VERSION®, NIV® Copyright © 1973, 1978, 1984,
2011 by Biblica, Inc.® Used by permission. All rights reserved worldwide.

Copyright Happiness Publishing, LLC

Copyright © 2014 Mike Duffy and Kendall Duffy
All Rights Reserved.

ISBN: 0692217479
ISBN 13: 9780692217474

The Happiness Book For Little Christians

A Biblical Guide To Happiness!

THE BIBLE

Kendall Duffy is in the third grade. She drew the pictures in this book. Her daddy, Mike Duffy wrote the words. God wrote the bible verses. They had a great time creating this book together. The bible is our instruction manual for happiness in life. Follow the teachings of the bible and you will be happier!

Here Are 14 Biblical Steps To Happiness:

1. Love God.
2. Love your neighbor like yourself.
3. Do not over-eat.
4. Give.
5. Don't Worry.
6. Honor your parents.
7. Be grateful.
8. Be kind.
9. Forgive.
10. Pray every day.
11. Do not be afraid.
12. Serve God.
13. Remember that God has a great plan for your life.
14. Memorize a favorite bible verse.

You can memorize the steps or just copy Kendall!

Kendall loves Jesus.

Matthew 22:37 (NASB) says, "You shall love the Lord your God with all your heart, and with all your soul, and with all your mind."

Kendall loves her family, friends and teachers.

Matthew 22:39 (NASB) says, "You shall love your neighbor as yourself."

Kendall doesn't over-eat.

Proverbs 25:16 (NASB) says
"...Eat only what you need..."

Kendall takes part of her allowance and gives it to charity.

2 Corinthians 9:7 (NASB) says "...God loves a cheerful giver."

Kendall doesn't worry.

Matthew 6:27 (NASB) says, "And who of you by being worried can add a single hour to his life?"

Kendall holds the door
open for her mommy.

Ephesians 6:2 (NASB) says,
"Honor your father and mother."

Kendall is grateful for everything given to her.

1 Thessalonians 5:18 (NASB) says "In everything give thanks; for this is God's will for you in Christ Jesus."

Kendall is kind to people.

Ephesians 4:32 (NASB) says, "Be kind to one another, tender-hearted..."

Kendall forgives her little brother, Mikey when he is bold to her.

Luke 6:37 (NIV) says, "...Forgive, and you will be forgiven."

Kendall Prays every night. She isn't afraid of the dark, because Jesus is the light of the world!

Isaiah 41:10 (NASB) says, "Do not fear, for I am with you; Do not anxiously look about you, for I am your God. I will strengthen you, surely I will help you, surely I will uphold you with My righteous right hand."

Serving God makes Kendall happy!

Ecclesiastes 2:26 (NIV) says, "To the person who pleases him, God gives wisdom, knowledge and happiness…"

Kendall has a favorite bible verse.

It is Jeremiah 29:11 (NIV) which says, "For I know the plans I have for you," declares the Lord, "plans to prosper you and not to harm you, plans to give you hope and a future."

What is your favorite bible verse?

Write it below and draw a picture about it on the next page.

_____

_____

_____

_____

_____

_____

Always remember that
Jesus loves you!

God Bless You!

About The Authors

Mike Duffy is the founder of Happiness Publishing, LLC. He has been researching happiness for over 29 years. He loves to write and speak about how you can gain greater happiness and joy in your wonderful and precious life. His audiences include corporations, universities and organizations. Mike is the founder of The Happiness Hall Of Fame. The Happiness Hall of Fame recognizes, encourages and celebrates people that through their talent, hard work and sacrifice make other people happy. www.happinesshalloffame.com

Kendall Duffy is in the third grade. She loves God and her family. She enjoys drawing, dancing, making her friends laugh, playing softball and singing in the choir.

www.ingramcontent.com/pod-product-compliance
Lightning Source LLC
Chambersburg PA
CBHW041537040426
42446CB00002B/131